EPIC SPOTS

THE PLACES YOU MUST SKATE BEFORE YOU DIE

WITHDRAWN

UNIVERSE

PUBLISHER Edward H Riggins
EDITOR IN CHIEF Jake Phelps
ASSISTANT PUBLISHER Jeff Rafnson
GENERAL COUNSEL James M Barrett

EDITOR AT LARGE Michael Burnett
MANAGING EDITOR Ryan Henry
CREATIVE DIRECTOR Kevin Convertito
ART DIRECTOR Dan Whiteley
ASSOCIATE ART DIRECTOR Adam Creagan
ASSOCIATE DESIGNER Trenton Temple
COPY EDITOR Erin Dyer

FILM SCAN TECH Randy Dodson
VIDEO ROAM Preston Maigetter
WEBSLINGER Greg Smith

STAFF PHOTOGRAPHERS
David Broach, Lance Dawes, Joe Hammeke,
Wez Lundry, Gabe Morford, Rhino, Rick Sanders

CONTRIBUTING PHOTOGRAPHERS
Jaya Bonderov, Kevin Convertito, Adam Conway,
Sean Cronan, Nik Freitas, Andy Harris, Travis Howell,
Zac Hudson, Bryce Kanights, Andrew Mapstone, Dan Mathieu,
Joey "Shigeo" Muellner, Ken Nagahara, Deville Nunes,
Patrick O'Dell, Luke Ogden, Scott Pommier, Giovanni Reda,
Rick Raymond, Nick Scurich, Michael Sieben, Tony Vitello,
Shelby Woods, Dan Zaslavsky, Tobin Yelland

WRITTEN BY
Michael Burnett, Jake Phelps, Ryan Henry, Adam Creagan

PHIL SHAO 1973–1998   RUBEN ORKIN 1969–1999   CURTIS HSIANG 1963–2000

First published in the United States of America in 2008
by UNIVERSE PUBLISHING
A Division of Rizzoli International Publications, Inc.
300 Park Avenue South
New York, NY 10010
www.rizzoliusa.com

© 2008 High Speed Productions, Inc.

2008 2009 2010 2011 2012 / 10 9 8 7 6 5 4 3 2 1

ISBN-13: 978-0-7893-1697-4

Library of Congress Catalog Control Number: 2007934241

HIGH SPEED PRODUCTIONS, INC.
1303 UNDERWOOD AVE., SAN FRANCISCO, CA, 94124
WWW.THRASHERMAGAZINE.COM

Chet Childress, frontside grind, Austria
Photo: Rhino

CONTENTS

Mike Peterson, boneless, Mammoth, CA
Photo: Luke Ogden

THE JOURNEY

SOME SAY that spots are like skaters themselves: Some hot, some not, some now, some gone forever. Skate it then split. If you happen to skate it again, so be it; if it gets bulldozed before your ride, too bad. There's more to skate and more to leave behind. Just keep moving, and the world will do the rest.
—*Jake Phelps*

Fullpipe somewhere in Texas
Photo: Luke Ogden

GREAT SKATE TOWNS

California
SAN FRANCISCO

The last town left. Come here and bomb a hill, muscle a burrito, and check the natural wonders of the Marin Headlands. SF, CA, Land's end.

Chad Fernandez, frontside noseslide
Photo: Jaya Bonderov

Erik Ellington, backside kickflip
Photo: Michael Burnett

California
LOS ANGELES

Once a desert, now a modern-day playground for millions. LA has it all: Handrails, movie stars, swimming pools, Governor Schwarzenegger…

Chad Muska, backside ollie
Photo: David Broach

Kristian Svitak, frontside bluntslide
Photo: Michael Burnett

New York

NEW YORK

Twelve million people can't
be wrong. Uptown, midtown,
downtown. August is hot as hell
and the pavement sweats.

Lewis Marnell, frontside 180
Photo: Andrew Mapstone

(opposite page)
Chris Trembly, backside lipslide
Photo: Patrick O'Dell

Arizona
PHOENIX

The desert that is Phoenix is hot, and the lizards that live there know how to rip. The pigs suck but the parks and pools are worth it.

David Gonzales, frontside kickflip
Photo: Joe Hammeke

(opposite page)
Leo Romero, backside tailslide
Photo: Michael Burnett

Florida
MIAMI

Down South on the wang, this city never sleeps. Downtown at night and on the beach by day? Fine indeed.

Darrell Stanton, pole-jam cannonball
Photo: Morf

(opposite page)
(L to R) **Gareth Stehr,**
Johnny Layton, Adrian Mallory
Photo: Michael Burnett

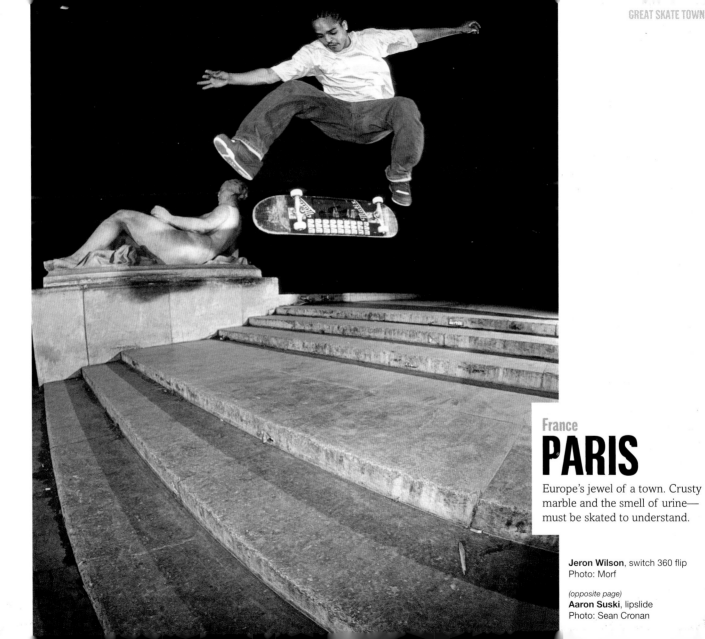

France
PARIS

Europe's jewel of a town. Crusty marble and the smell of urine—must be skated to understand.

Jeron Wilson, switch 360 flip
Photo: Morf

(opposite page)
Aaron Suski, lipslide
Photo: Sean Cronan

Spain

BARCELONA

Spanish Inquisitors need only push around to see how a city was meant to be. Ledges, hills, parks; you name it, Barcelona's got it.

Diego Bucchieri, ollie crail grab
Photo: Michael Burnett

(opposite page)
Bryan Herman, frontside kickflip
Photo: Patrick O'Dell

Colorado
DENVER

High Plains Drifters know that
the Mile High City has pretty
much everything you need.

Andrew Reynolds, ollie
Photo: Lance Dawes

John Cardiel, slappy 5-0
Photo: Michael Burnett

EPIC SKATE PARKS

Washington
ORCAS ISLAND

The last for now of Red and Monk together.
The ferry ride to the island makes it worth it.

Peter Hewitt, lien air
Photo: Joe Hammeke

(opposite page)
Photo: Kevin Convertito

Gold Coast, Australia
PIZZEY BOWL

Pizzey is, quite frankly, one gnar place to ride a skateboard. Kinked, two channels, and rougher than Alicia Keyes' face make it all or nothing.

Matt Mumford, boneless
Photo: Michael Burnett

Shane Cross, backside noseblunt
Photo: Rhino

Japan
LOST RUINS

Built by aliens, never skated, it awaits your turn until they tear it down or the snow bears eat it up—whichever comes first. Killer bowl into a 150-foot-long halfpipe.

Remy Stratton, frontside rock
Photo: Luke Ogden

(opposite page)
Photo: Luke Ogden

China
SHANGHAI

The largest park in the world is also the loneliest. Miles and hits for generations to come.

Rune Glifberg, backside Smith
Photo: Michael Burnett

Omar Hassan, judo air
Photo: Joe Hammeke

Florida
KONA

One of the oldest in America
that's still in existence,
Jacksonville's concrete will still be
here long after Iran wins the war.

Mike Peterson, lien air
Photo: Rhino

California
MAMMOTH

Built in the rocks and the cool
mountain air. Kinda sketchy,
but massive.

Matt Mumford, backside Smith
Photo: Luke Ogden

Kentucky
LOUISVILLE

Double Black Diamond territory. Initial design flaws led to some early deaths, but that's what parks are for—scaring the crap out of you.

Shane Cross, frontside feeble grind
Photo: Michael Burnett

Diego Bucchieri, frontside carve
Photo: Michael Burnett

Cayman Islands
BLACK PEARL

The Cayman Islands skatepark is supposedly built entirely on Red Stripe beer bottles. Coral coping and endless lines—ask Rune

Matt Dove, crooked grind
Photo: Rhino

(opposite page)
Steve Bailey, invert
Photo: Rhino

Ecuador
QUITO

Blackouts, floods, gangs, thieves, and revolution. Damn…Sounds like fun, until you have to go to the hospital. Huge park in the middle of an even bigger park; gnarledocious.

Keegan Sauder, method
Photo: Michael Burnett

(opposite page)
Peter Hewitt, frontside grind
Photo: Rhino

Oregon
KLAMATH FALLS

Built on a landfill, Klamath has got a lot of terrain—from tweaked-out teenagers to down-hill ski jumps. A must for all Oregon-bound 'boarders.

Lance Mountain, invert
Photo: Michael Burnett

Matt Mumford, frontside tailbone
Photo: Michael Burnett

Oregon
LINCOLN CITY

Redneck built this and liked it so
much that he moved in to town.
They keep adding on; now there's
a pool and a cradle, and the
Dairy Queen is about as far as
you can throw a rock.

Karma Tsocheff, *frontside grind*
Photo: Luke Ogden

Brian Seber, frontside rock
Photo: Luke Ogden

Japan
ANAKA

Smooth, green, and bad, Anaka bowl is one of the best five pits in the world. Concrete coping and a deep channel make it top drawer.

Rune Glifberg, frontside air
Photo: Luke Ogden

(opposite page)
Pete Colpitts, frontside grind
Photo: Luke Ogden

Kettering, Ohio
DC SKATE PLAZA

Skate plazas could be the wave of the future, or not. The siren song of the raw streets will always call, but the no-hassle factor sure counts.

Shane Cross, bluntslide
Photo: Michael Burnett

France
MARSEILLE

Built in 1990, Marsy was one of the first—and still worth a five-hour train ride from Paris on the SNCF to the sunny Mediterranean. Topless beach, but watch your stuff; the thugs run the sand.

Dylan Reider, no-comply tailslide
Photo: Rhino

(opposite page)
Tony Trujillo, lien air
Photo: Michael Burnett

REEDSPORT

Kill graff (not), weird lines, and good
Oregon fun. Mini-ramp skills won't
help you here.

Jeff Grosso, Andrecht
Photo: Michael Burnett

John Rattray, tailgrab fakie
Photo: Michael Burnett

Oregon
ASTORIA

Judging by Peter's screaming,
it must be fun.

Peter Hewitt, stalefish
Photo: Joe Hammeke

ALGORTA

Basque country. An old biscuit rejuiced with a killer pool in an ancient Spanish castle.

Alain Goikoetxea, frontside nosegrind
Photo: Joe Hammeke

(opposite page)
Photo: Joe Hammeke

Colorado
CARBONDALE

Nestled in the middle of nowhere,
the park awaits. The Summer of
2004 is one they'll never forget.

Al Partanen, lipslide
Photo: Luke Ogden

(opposite page)
Photo: Michael Burnett

Idaho
HAILEY

Red built this; there are parts that nobody will ever grind. Right next to a rodeo rink for drunk kicks.

Peter Hewitt, boneless
Photo: Tobin Yelland

Colorado
DENVER

Denver is a gnarly place, and this park is no exception. Slippery when dusty, along with the altitude, make it both a workout and dangerous.

Mike Vallely, frontside invert
Photo: Luke Ogden

THE SHOWBOWL

Mexico
BAJA BOWL

Yeah, you might have a bowl like this not far from your house. But you can only get the gorgeous Mexican coastline in one place.

Steve Bailey, frontside grind
Photo: Luke Ogden

(opposite page)
Than Brooks, frontside air
Photo: Andy Harris

GNAR ZONE

WALLENBERG

They just put in a handicap ramp at Wallenberg. From Paez to Gerwer to Reynolds, the history in the Big Four runs deep.

Andrew Reynolds, backside kickflip
Photo: Dan Zaslavsky

(opposite page)
Mark Gonzales, ollie
Photo: Michael Burnett

San Diego, CA
RINCON

A massive Big Four and a precarious rail with head-high drop off makes this one of Southern California's gnarliest proving grounds. At Rincon, it's get it right or get broke off.

Josh Harmony, frontside nosegrind
Photo: Michael Burnett

Chris Dobstaff, nollie heelflip
Photo: Nick Scurich

CARLSBAD

Carlsbad's been hot and cold over
the years. Land a trick and ride into
the grass—and who can forget
Jeremy Wray in *Second Hand Smoke*?

Johnny Layton, switch 360 flip
Photo: Michael Burnett

Hollywood, CA
HOLLYWOOD HIGH

The most famous set of rails in the world, Hollywood attracts the hordes from far and wide who want to take a tech trick to the 12 or become a hero tangling with the 16.

Shane Cross, salad grind
Photo: Nick Scurich

Jon Allie, stalefish
Photo: Shigeo

Orange County, CA

EL TORO

Heath Kirchart broke this monster in, while daredevils from the world over continue to get broke off on its 20 steep stairs. Be the first to land a trick at The Bull and you can claim a piece of skate history.

Don Nguyen, ollie
Photo: Michael Burnett

CAIRO'S SPOT

This drop is a beast for sure.
Downtown O-Town is a
ghost town on the weekends.
Go and rip it if you can.

Cairo Foster, nosegrind
Photo: Dan Zaslavsky

San Francisco, CA

CLIPPER

A little rounded, a little slick, the Clipper ledge has seen mind-blowing moves by everyone from Mark Appleyard to Darrell Stanton.

Jon Allie, kickflip tailslide
Photo: Morf

San Francisco, CA

LINCOLN

Lincoln has made some people quite rich: Think Jim Greco's switch frontside flick. Then there's Jeremy Wray, and nobody can fade Andrew Reynolds for this kind of thing.

Andrew Reynolds, backside nollie 180
Photo: Luke Ogden

San Francisco, CA

HUBBA HIDEOUT

Hubba Hideout was named by James Kelch in the early '90s. Businessmen who worked nearby would come and smoke rock under the bridge. Lennie Kirk and Fred Gall had some of the first bangers.

Jack Curtin, switch backside lipslide
Photo: Dan Zaslavsky

VARSITY PLAZA

This stack, situated on Australia's Gold Coast,
was the site of the world's biggest backside 360
when local Chima Ferguson spun and stuck one.
Since then, it's hosted a professional event,
a security crackdown, and a few lucky
sessions by those in the know.

Paul Rodriguez, varial heelflip
Photo: Michael Burnett

San Francisco, CA

CALIFORNIA STREET

California Street is very steep. This gap's at the top, so when you land it, ride or die.

Abdias Rivera, ollie
Photo: Nick Scurich

(opposite page)
Justin Brock, 360 flip
Sequence: Morf

SPORTS ARENA TRIPLE-SET

This low and long triple-set has an esteemed skate video history. The ABD list still has a few holes in it, though.

Pat Rakestraw, tailslide
Photo: Michael Burnett

Oceanside, CA
O-SIDE HUBBA

Right by the beach in Oceanside is a tall-ass hubba where you can either impress the chicks or sign up for a visit to the local hospital.

Johnny Layton, nosegrind
Photo: Michael Burnett

PRIVATE FACILITIES

Vista, CA
BOB'S COMPLEX

Bob built this retreat so he could reinvent skateboarding on his own time. The cork screw, loop, fullpipe, and monster vert ramp all play warm-up for his latest toy—the diabolical Mega Ramp.

Bob Burnquist, loop flip
Photo: Luke Ogden

(opposite page)
Photo: Luke Ogden

Arizona
ROWLEY'S RAMP

Some pros like to get away from it all, so they build little facilities out in the middle of nowhere. Rowley's ramp is top secret.

Arto Saari, frontside kickflip
Photo: Michael Burnett

Costa Mesa, CA
RVCA RAMP

Part art gallery, part backyard bowl, the RVCA ramp is where the OC's skaters, surfers, and doodlers come together to compare haircuts and hit the lip.

Brent Atchley, lien
Photo: Michael Burnett

Stu Graham, low-to-high grind
Photo: Michael Burnett

Vista, CA
BLACK BOX FACILITY

A team as fearsome as Zero needs an equally mean clubhouse. The Black Box park has everything a modern street warrior could want, with simulated rails, ledges, and hubbas littering the expansive space.

Tony Cervantes, frontside air
Photo: Michael Burnett

John Rattray, dog pisser
Photo: Shigeo

LEGENDARY POOLS

Los Angeles, CA
PINK MOTEL

In *Animal Chin*, the owner told the Bones Brigade they could do "whatever you want in there, if you want." These days, this mellow, whale-shaped pool is skateable only to those with money to spend.

Lance Mountain air over **Salba**
Photo: Luke Ogden

(opposite page)
Anthony Van Engelen, frontside grind
Photo: Michael Burnett

Cambridge, MA

CAMBRIDGE

An East Coast standby, this Boston bowl has a harsh kink to vert and a slick, square lip. Frank "The Wrecka" Lannon was an early hero, and Charlie Wilkins stills tears it. Don't go in the summer. It's filled with water.

John Cardiel, backside air
Photo: Luke Ogden

Kyle Berard, backside Smith
Photo: Rhino

Jon Allie, crailslide
Photo: Shigeo

Strawberry, CA
STRAWBERRY

On a windy road to Lake Tahoe, the Strawberry Lodge tempts all who pass it. A new lip in the late '90s made it 100 times better, but shaky, ever-changing owners threatened its future. This just in...it got dozed.

Diego Bucchieri, backside lipslide
Photo: Michael Burnett

Fresno, CA

VAGABOND

Los Tigres Del Norte shut this hotel down, but the skaters kept the pool alive for almost 10 years—even going so far as to add concrete curves to the decks before the city finally filled the whole thing.

Lance Mountain, backside air
Photo: Michael Burnett

Omar Hasan, 540
Photo: Lance Dawes

Albany, NY
ALBANY

A closely-guarded secret, this mellow one-hitter is on a strict need-to-know basis despite being sessioned for the past 20 years.

Bill Danforth, frontside rock
Photo: Lance Dawes

Silas Baxter-Neal, backside noseblunt
Photo: Lance Dawes

SICK STREET SPOTS

San Francisco, CA
3RD & ARMY

When they built it they busted skating hard there, but now it's all good. A no-hassle dream spot.

Jerry Smythe, frontside crooked grind
Photo: Tony Vitello

(opposite page)
Brian Anderson, ollie
Photo: Rick Raymond

San Francisco, CA

PIER 7

When EMB got zorched, skaters just went down the street to Pier 7. It became a laboratory for manual and ledge-work lunacy. It's still there and skateable, sort of.

Stevie Williams, nollie 180 heelflip to fakie nose manual 180 out
Sequence: Shelby Woods

New York, NY

BROOKLYN BANKS

Of all the spots featured in this book, one of the most recognizable is the Brooklyn Banks. These bricks have been waiting for you for over 100 years.

Rick Howard, wallride crail
Photo: Michael Burnett

Josh Maready, rock fakie
Photo: Patrick O'Dell

INFAMOUS MINI RAMPS

Long Beach, CA
ALMOST RAMP

Cheese and Crackers put this kind of Marx Brothers-like skating on the map. Mini-ramps come and go; this one did.

Daewon Song, ollie nosegrind fakie
Photo: Reda

(opposite page)
Chris Haslam, frontside grind
Photo: Reda

Oakland, CA
JIM'S RAMP

Oakland, Bitch! In an industrial wasteland, Thiebaud built his own dreamscape. Now it's your turn—start lookin.'

Julien Stranger, frontside grind
Photo: Zac Hudson

SUNSHINE COAST

Solidly built and always a blast.
When you skate here you'll be
putting on a beach-dweller demo,
so have your stock tricks ready
to roll...then go for a swim.

Matt Mumford, fastplant fakie
Photo: Andrew Mapstone

Austin, TX
BANANA FARM

The ramp you wish you grew up with. If you lurk up on their scene just say you know Michael Sieben.

Johnny Layton, backside disaster
Photo: Michael Burnett

(opposite page)
Photo: Rhino

DITCH
DESTINATIONS

SOUTHWEST ^{USA}

The Southwest is criss-crossed by concrete spillways at the ready in case of flood. The other 364 days of the year they sit bone dry, ready to shred.

Arto Saari, frontside wallride
Photo: Michael Burnett

(opposite page)
John Ponts, ollie into bank
Photo: Rhino

Southern California

MYSTERY DITCH

It may be a federal offense, but that doesn't stop thrill seekers from taking a chance at this massive pit high above San Diego.

John White, frontside kickflip
Photo: Deville Nunes

Albuquerque, NM
INDIAN SCHOOL

Get dropped off high in the hills and enjoy a no-push downhill slide that lasts over 20 minutes. Albuquerque's Indian School is one of the seven great skate wonders of the world.

SAD, frontside grind
Photo: Scott Pommier

(opposite page)
Photo: Rhino

Alhambra, CA

ALHAMBRA

Take it over the hip and you're
in for the ride of your life at this
steep, mountain-top plunge.

Arto Saari, frontside half-Cab kickflip
Photo: Michael Burnett

Hawaii
WALLOS

In the steep mountains of Oahu, this mythical spillway is as rough as it is quick. Watch your ass, Haole! Wallos will eat you alive.

Sam Clemens, frontside slob
Photo: Michael Burnett

Los Angeles, CA
SKIP'S DITCH

Where street skating meets ditch, this paved stretch of the Santa Ana river has more spots than 100 skateparks put together.

Chad Bartie, frontside blunt
Photo: Michael Burnett

Houston, TX
EZ-7

Named because you can easily hit the lip seven times in a run, this ditch has extensions, a channel, parking blocks, and a nearby river that's claimed more boards than bad report cards.

Matt Mumford, noseblunt
Photo: Michael Burnett

(opposite page)
Wayne Patrick, ollie
Photo: Travis Howell

John Rattray, kickflip
Photo: Michael Burnett

California
TEMECULA

So-Cal sprawl has spawned hundreds of new bank spots, but this Temecula gem is one of the best.

Stu Graham, boneless
Photo: Michael Burnett

Salba, frontside thruster
Photo: Luke Ogden

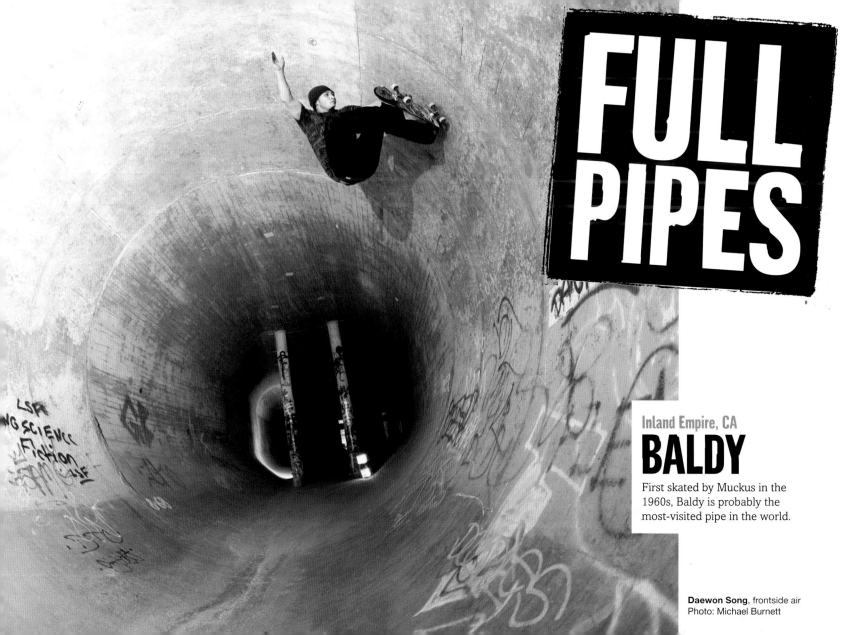

FULL PIPES

Inland Empire, CA
BALDY

First skated by Muckus in the 1960s, Baldy is probably the most-visited pipe in the world.

Daewon Song, frontside air
Photo: Michael Burnett

Auckland, New Zealand
HUIA PIPE

Climbing into this fungal stew is
not for the faint of heart. One slip
and you go home in a pine box.

Tony Trujillo, *frontside carve*
Photo: Luke Ogden

Northern California
GLORY HOLE

Large wheels make it more fun;
road weapons make it lethal. Miss
the pump and you lose the juice.

Alan Petersen, frontside ollie
Photo: Luke Ogden

UNIQUE SPOTS

Corona, CA
BATTLE BOWL

After wrecking so many of our ledges, the least the BMXers can do is share the Battle Bowl with us. Even if we tell you this spot is outside of Corona, California, you will never, ever find it.

Kevin Long, frontside air
Photo: Lance Dawes

(opposite page)
Austin Stephens, backside crailslide
Photo: Michael Burnett

San Francisco, CA

CHINA BANKS

Syringes, band-aids, broken bones—
it's all here. Lots of feelings have
been hurt at the banks. Many have
tried; gnar-zone to the max.

Julien Stranger, frontside ollie
Photo: Bryce Kanights

(opposite page)
Dan Drehobl, mute fakie
Photo: Luke Ogden

Chicago, IL

SEA WALL

Situated below Shedd's Aquarium, this smooth curve is mere feet from the choppy waters of Lake Michigan.

Steve Fauser, backside carve
Photo: Adam Conway

Tony Trujillo, roll-in
Photo: Morf

San Francisco, CA

FORT MILEY

Go there and see how hard it is to ollie the big hip. Brian Ferdinand ripped it, but Phil Shao, well...it's a whole new ball game. Good place to see the end of the world.

Phil Shao, grind
Photo: Luke Ogden

SLANT GAP

A dangerous spot, and not just because you might fall through the windows—the cops at this Denver, Colorado slant have a zero-tolerance policy.

Nick Dompierre, ollie
Photo: Morf

PALA PIPES

In an orchard near the Pala Indian Casino, these tubes give daredevils a chance to get looped and gap from flume to flume.

Rodney Jones, blindside kickflip
Photo: Rhino

(opposite page)
Ben Raybourn, crail air
Photo: Michael Burnett

Central Texas
TEXAS WAVE

Good luck skating this fantastic three-quarterpipe. You have to build a dam to keep the water at bay.

Chet Childress, frontside grind
Photo: Rhino

(opposite page)
Punker Matt, frontside air
Photo: Joe Hammeke

Tempe, AZ

THE WEDGE

Tempe, Arizona's The Wedge has a hubba, banks, and even a crappy concrete skatepark, making this a must-shred for anyone on an AZ mission.

Diego Bucchieri, frontside bluntslide
Photo: Michael Burnett

(opposite page)
Steve Fauser, noseslide
Photo: Adam Conway

San Jose, CA
DEL'S WALL

San Jose legends from Jason Adams
to Stevie Cab have busted Berts and
flipped to fakie on this mellow butte.

Jason Adams, boardslide
Photo: Rhino

BIG SURF

They hosted a pro contest in the '80s, but these days the only way you'll get to skate this AZ water-park is with a permission slip.

Kris Markovich, crooked cop
Photo: Michael Burnett

San Diego, CA

HEDDINGS' HIP

Rough 'crete in a rough San Diego neighborhood, it took a skater as tough as Neil Heddings to break in this gnarly nubbin.

Zarosh Eggleston, noseblunt drop-in
Photo: Rhino

(opposite page)
Johnny Layton, method
Photo: Michael Burnett

Montreal, Canada
THE BIG O

Built for the 1976 Olympics in Montreal, this perfect mini-ramp is actually an entrance to an unused stadium. Barry Walsh and Marc Tisson are the local heavies.

Tom Penny, kickflip fakie
Photo: Michael Burnett

(opposite page)
Barry Walsh, backside air
Photo: Dan Mathieu

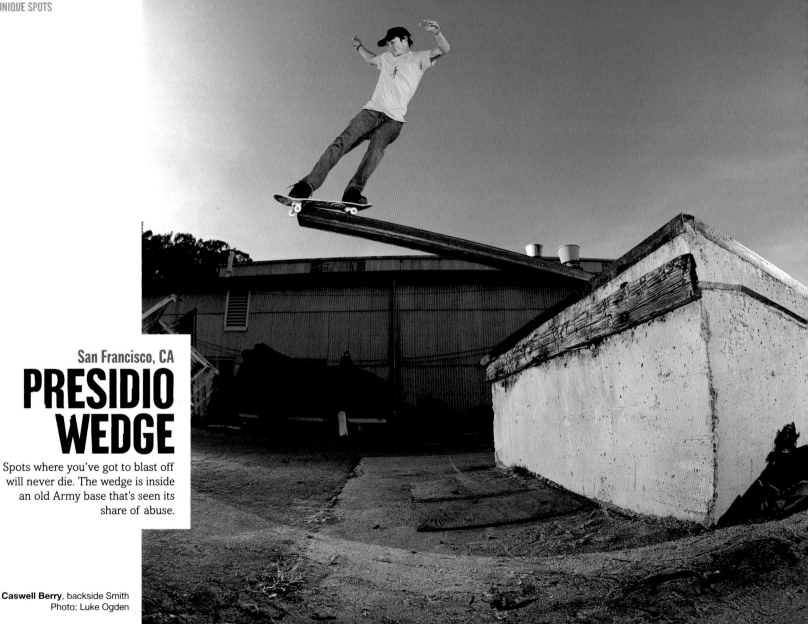

San Francisco, CA

PRESIDIO WEDGE

Spots where you've got to blast off will never die. The wedge is inside an old Army base that's seen its share of abuse.

Caswell Berry, backside Smith
Photo: Luke Ogden

Scott Kane, frontside half-Cab kickflip
Photo: Tony Vitello

Northern California
THE HOOK

Jumping fences is the best part of skating. Being where you aren't supposed to be makes the rush just that much more gnar. Two-hundred-fifty-dollar tickets? So it goes.

Errol Langdon, frontside air
Photo: Ken Nagahara

(opposite page)
Curtis Hsiang, frontside carve
Photo: Bryce Kanights

BUILD YOUR OWN

Portland, OR

BURNSIDE

What started as a lump of concrete against a bank under Portland's Burnside bridge has spawned a Do-It-Yourself concrete revolution. Still one of the fastest, scariest, and punkest parks on the planet.

Peter Hewitt, nosegrind
Photo: Joe Hammeke

(opposite page)
Clint Peterson, lien air
Photo: Shelby Woods

Sam Hitz, frontside boardslide
Photo: Rhino

San Diego, CA
WASHINGTON STREET

A respite from up-tight San Diego, Washington Street is loose as a goose with the rules, but steep and deep with the 'crete. Bring your slashing skills and an open mind to get the most out of this pit.

Matt Dove, blunt fakie
Photo: Rhino

San Pedro, CA

CHANNEL STREET

Built by longshoremen in the shadow
of the Port of LA, San Pedro's
Channel Street adds a twist to the DIY
concrete formula: namely, friendly
locals and a no-vibes atmosphere.
This park could be your life.

Steve Bailey, frontside pivot
Photo: Luke Ogden

(opposite page)
John Rattray, crailtap
Photo: Michael Burnett

Philadelphia, PA
FDR

A rip-roaring concrete curl in the heart of the ultra-dope East Coast skate scene, the street skaters pretend FDR doesn't exist while the locals battle BMXers to ride this ever-changing gem.

Chet Childress, frontside feeble grind
Photo: Rhino

(opposite page)
Photo: Luke Ogden

Hawaii
CHOLO'S

Perched on Oahu's infamous
North Shore, Cholo built his own epic
wave in the form of a killer amoeba.

Jeff Grosso, boneless
Photo: Joe Hammeke

(opposite page)
Omar Hassan, 5-0 fakie
Photo: Joe Hammeke

Rutland, Ohio
SKATOPIA

If the Beverly Hillbillies had rolled all that Texas Tea money into a sprawling skate farm, it might look something like Skatopia. Concrete, wood, steel, and acres of beer-drenched mud make this a thrash destination for the truly adventurous.

Rick McCrank, backside lipslide
Photo: Luke Ogden

Rune Glifberg, frontside heelflip
Photo: Scott Pommier

Seattle, WA
WEST SEATTLE BOWL

After injuring all his friends with his first bowl next door, Monk made it right with the ultra-smooth Butter Bowl in his own backyard.

Mark Hubbard, backside ollie
Photo: Luke Ogden

(opposite page)
Mark Hubbard, long exposure line
Photo: Wez Lundry

WORLD WIDE RIDE

ARGENTINA

The Europe of South America mixes modern architecture with good ol' Old World grime to spawn a skate maze that'll challenge all comers.

Diego Bucchieri, stalefish
Photo: Rhino

(opposite page)
Danny Fuenzalida, tailslide
Photo: Dan Zaslavsky

UNITED KINGDOM

After the USA, the UK has the most true Thrashers. Rough cobblestone and ancient parks just make the air time and crooked grinds that much sweeter.

Devine Calloway, 5-0
Photo: Michael Burnett

Al Partanen, frontside blunt
Photo: Joe Hammeke

JAPAN

The cops are so polite in Japan, you won't even realize they're telling you to leave. Marble and polished granite is spread liberally around Tokyo, while some ancient parks are tapped by those in the know.

Jerry Hsu, pivot fakie
Photo: Patrick O'Dell

Hachi, frontside grind
Photo: Luke Ogden

Keegan Sauder, kickflip
Photo: Michael Burnett

PERU

Lush jungle gives way to some of the harshest cities since *Mad Max*. The spots in Peru can be a challenge, but the local skaters are some of the coolest in the world.

Johnny Layton, Smith grind
Photo: Michael Burnett

NEW ZEALAND

A kinder, gentler Australia,
New Zealand has sheep, scenery,
and laid back skaters ready to share
their wealth of awesome parks
and hidden street spots.

John Cardiel, boneless
Photo: Luke Ogden

(opposite page)
Tony Trujillo, frontside boardslide
Photo: Luke Ogden

COSTA RICA

This surfer's paradise has a little bit to offer to the sidewalk shredders, too. Hidden bowls, a few crusty street spots, and 365 days of sun make Costa Rica a skate destination for those who mostly want to lie on the beach.

Dan Pensyl, ollie fakie
Photo: Joe Hammeke

(opposite page)
Chet Childress, backside disaster
Photo: Joe Hammeke

UNITED ARAB EMIRATES

A Muslim Las Vegas on the tip of the Arabian Peninsula, Dubai's building boom churns out spots on a daily basis. Grab your gold card and get there (if you can afford it).

Aaron Suski, stalefish
Photo: Lance Dawes

(opposite page)
Aaron Suski, 360 flip
Photo: Lance Dawes

POLAND

Behind the Iron Curtain lies a
wealth of awesome street spots.
Poland is another country where
skating is on a serious rise.

Dennis Busenitz, frontside ollie
Photo: Joe Hammeke

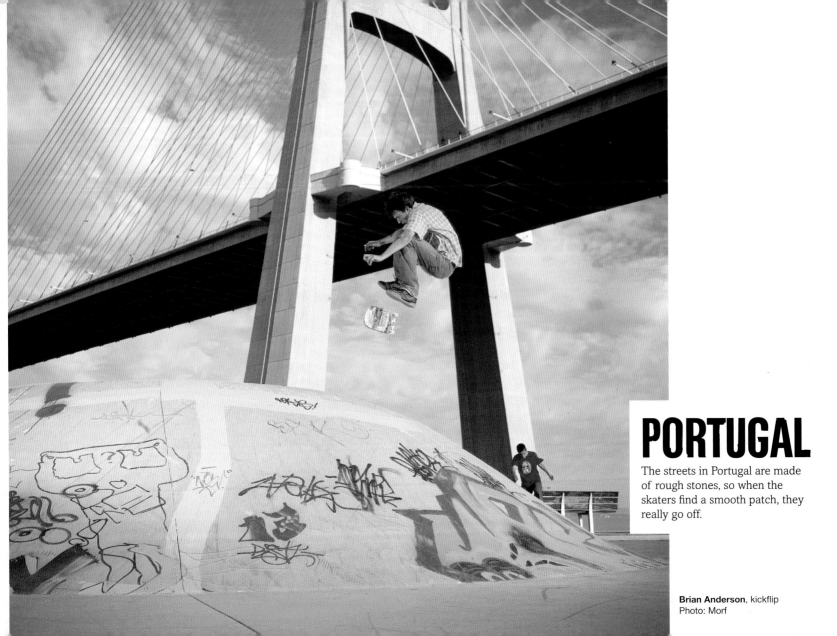

PORTUGAL

The streets in Portugal are made of rough stones, so when the skaters find a smooth patch, they really go off.

Brian Anderson, kickflip
Photo: Morf

MEXICO

Bring your big wheels and an open mind—Mexico has tons of less-than-perfect spots, but a growing skate scene with many friendly locals.

Angel Ramirez, kickflip
Photo: Michael Burnett

Brian Heck, crailtap
Photo: Luke Ogden

SOUTH AFRICA

Skate Camp in the middle of grass huts and villagers with real spears. Zulu Village is about as remote as you can get.

Darrell Stanton, stalefish to fakie
Photo: Luke Ogden

Remy Stratton, crail air
Photo: Luke Ogden

CHINA

The new frontier, China is building spots 10 times faster than the cops in California are taking them away. Marble for miles and the locals are too stoked to kick you out.

David Gonzales, noseblunt slide
Photo: Michael Burnett

(opposite page)
Rodrigo Teixeira, 50-50
Photo: Michael Burnett

RUSSIA

In the Soviet times, skaters in Russia had to make their own trucks. These days, anything goes, as once-sacred marble monuments become prime skate spots.

Rick Howard, kickflip wallride
Photo: Michael Burnett

ULTIMATE SKATE DESTINATION

AUSTRALIA

It's far, but it's worth it. Once you're there, get a pie and a beer and sit on the beach and remember it for the rest of your life.

Chris Senn, feeble grind
Photo: Michael Burnett

Shane Cross, backside ollie
Photo: Rhino

Darrell Stanton, switch kickflip
Photo: Luke Ogden

(opposite page)
Matt Mumford, stalefish
Photo: Andrew Mapstone

SKATE EVERY THING

YOUR BACKYARD

Property ownership is part of the
American Dream. Put in a ramp back
there and you're good to go.
Expect guests. Lots of them.

Scott Taylor, Madonna
Photo: Michael Burnett

(opposite page)
Chad Shetler, backside noseblunt
Photo: Dan Zaslavsky

THE ROOF

Don't forget to look up once in awhile. You may be surprised at what you find. However, wheelbite takes on a new meaning when you're up top.

Jake Palu, kickflip
Photo: Tony Vitello

Ryan Bobier, backside kickflip
Photo: Shigeo

POOLS

Empty pools are the crown jewels of skateboarding. However, they require research, hard work, blind luck, and sometimes felony trespassing charges.

Jimmy Moore, frontside grind
Photo: Michael Burnett

GAPS

All you've got to do is get from here to there. It's the exact same ollie mechanics you've done a million times. Easy, right?

Van Wastell, ollie
Photo: Michael Burnett

RAILS

One of the craziest, biggest-risk, highest pay-off thrills in skating. They've always been there but it took Natas and Mark Gonzales to open the floodgates.

David Gravette, 50-50
Photo: Joe Hammeke

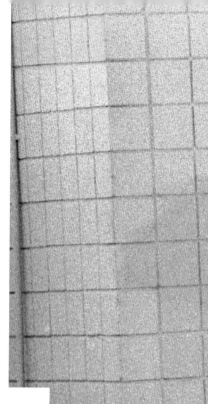

DOWN THE STREET

It could be a street you've never seen or it could be the one you grew up on. It doesn't matter. Somewhere between your board hitting the ground and that first push, the spot hunt has already begun.

Steve Nesser, ollie
Photo: Nik Freitas

THE DESTINATION

FORTUNATELY, the best spots haven't been skated (or even built) yet. This book should either get you hyped for it or make you quit. Get moving...
—*Jake Phelps*

Louie Barletta, 5-0
Photo: Patrick O'Dell

(last page)
Hunting for spots
Photo: Nick Scurich